A HOW-TO GUIDE for...

AUTOMATIC "TRANCE" WRITING
The
POWER to RECEIVE
MESSAGES
From BEYOND!

By GINA CANNONE
Psychic Medium

Author of "It's Time To Believe" in Angels, Spirit Guides
and Yourself

IbbiLane Press
copyright © 2017

ISBN-13: 978-0692873960 (IbbiLane Press)

ISBN-10: 0692873961

DEDICATION

*This book is dedicated to all those who have supported
me through the years and believe
there is life after life...*

*and I believe
the gifts to communicate with spirit
is in all of us...*

*Bringing us peace and enlightenment...
looking at all life with new eyes!*

The purpose of this book is to show how we can
communicate with our loved ones
after they are gone,
believing in the messages that are sent,
that can bring peace and guidance.

FOREWORD

Genuine…Inspirational…Nurturing…Altruistic…

I met Gina in class, as one of her students in her Past Life Regression Certification program. Listening and taking in her way of doing hypnotherapy, I learned more than just techniques. I learned about myself. I learned about courage and faith. I learned about Angels and Spirit Guides, hope, and letting go.

Gina is genuine, authentic, sincere, brave and real. She is inspirational and smart and a beacon of light to those who heed her words. All one has to do is read her first book; "It's Time to Believe" in Angels, Spirit Guides and Yourself, to learn about her faith and resilience-blessed with strength that is rooted in God's love.

Gina is nurturing and encouraging. She cares. Instilling hope where there is none.

Gina is Altruistic-Selfless-Fearless. Concerned about the wellness of others and focused on the greater good. Like the Angels and Spirit Guides she converses with and speaks about, she too is a Messenger, an Ambassador of the Good.

She is blessed and gifted with psychic abilities which she offers to the service of the greater good.

This book; AUTOMATIC TRANCE WRITING, The Power to Receive Messages From Beyond, is Gina's second book. It is her goal and intention to help those who are open to the spirit world to learn how to communicate with Angels and Spirit Guides, who are all around us to help us and guide us. It is labor of love Gina shares with her readers, how much we are blessed, loved and supported by Angels and Spirit Guides.

In this book, Gina reveals the way she dialogues with Spirit through Automatic Writing. This is another way how altruistic she is, by handing you the key to communicate- so that you can draw from strengths or gifts you have, that perhaps you're not aware of yet.

May you, the reader, be blessed and inspired in the same way I feel blessed to have met Gina.

Marcel Tabone
Clinical Psychologist

TESTIMONIALS

I walked into my reading with Gina with an open mind and walked out absolutely amazed by her accuracy! You see, my mom saw Gina for the first time about a month earlier. I knew I wanted to go within the next few weeks, so I told my mom not to mention me AT ALL and thankfully, she didn't. Gina told my mom things about me, my family, etc., that there was NO WAY she would have known about, she even drew pictures of a vegetable garden that's brand new and we all love. Well, fast forward about a month later and I met Gina for my reading. Knowing that she knew nothing about my connection to my mom, I was curious about what she would say. When Gina does a reading, she writes and draws images. Little did I know, after about a minute in, she started telling me the EXACT same things she told my mom a month earlier. Oh, and that vegetable garden drawing I mentioned a minute ago, came up in mine!! She connected with the spirits in a way that makes you truly know that she is doing what she was put on this earth to do. Her connection with the spirits is one that I have never seen anyone else have; her gift is one that you do not see often.

Gina B.

"Gina Cannone is like a secret treasure chest of priceless gems! Anyone who is lucky enough to find her will have an assortment of jewels to choose from - hypnotherapy, clairvoyant psychic readings, mediumship readings, spiritual life coaching, and live experiential workshops to develop your own skills. I have done them all! Not only is Gina amazingly accurate with her psychic information, she is generous, patient, and totally non-judgmental with her direct, yet sensitive style and warm personality. Everything about Gina is *authentic*. She is *the real deal* as a psychic, and the real deal as a compassionate, honest human being. Her live workshops are fun and informative, and you always leave better than when you came in. Gina has a gift for understanding your situation, and her hypnotherapy sessions are custom designed to your specific situation and needs, and help you quickly overcome any subconscious blocks that might be keeping you from moving forward in your life. She is a rare and priceless gem indeed!"

Melissa A.

I first met Gina when I picked up her business card. I became intrigued with all her abilities. I kept looking at her card and after a few days I called her. She was delightful. The first thing she told me was do not tell her anything about myself except my first name. I knew I wanted to see her. I made an appointment that week. The reading was right on. She told me things that there was no way she could have known. I have been to many psychics in my lifetime; I would say she was the best medium, psychic that I have been to see. She discussed my family with me especially my daughter. She said things to me that there was no way she could have known. I told my daughter about the reading and she called Gina and made an appointment. I *never told* Gina that my daughter was coming to see her.
When my daughter met with Gina she told her exactly the same thing she told me about herself. That was it! I knew I found the right person.

M. Greenberg

"BTW. I spoke to my mother after my reading and she told me things I didn't know -but that you said and wrote it within your automatic writings during the reading. So you are RIGHT ON!"

D.H.

AUTHOR'S PREFACE

The amazing and automatic "trance" writings that I do during each private session have brought much peace and happiness to both my clients and myself. As a psychic medium, I don't need to automatic write, but my gifts seem to be stronger when I do. This book is about communicating with spirit through the writing process. Why it works, how it works and what the messages, symbols and drawings actually mean.

The chapters in this book are from my own experiences with automatic "trance" writing. Real samples of my automatic writings will show how spirit comes through with many words, pictures and symbols. I never know what is going to appear on paper and am equally excited to see the outcome of every session.

Being that I am a board certified clinical hypnotherapist, it is extremely easy for me to put myself in a "trance" state. I seldom remember the details of any of my reading sessions, being that I am in a relaxed light trance state.

This book will guide and teach you how to properly begin communicating with spirit. It is an easy form of communication with spirit, that you can practice and get skilled at. It is also wonderful to have a tangible piece of evidence of what spirit has passed through you to write. Learning to become open and enter a trance state of mind is key to successful automatic writing. Letting the subconscious take over and accept and write whatever comes to mind, both good and bad.

Automatic trance writing is an amazing and enlightening form of intuitiveness that anyone can try for themselves. I have taught this technique in many of my workshops, and even if slow at first, with practice, it becomes easier, clearer and quicker to communicate.

This book is for those who want to learn about automatic trance writing and for those who may actually want to experience it for themselves. Even clients, who were skeptical about this process, had a complete change of heart after one of my sessions.

My goal is for everyone to experience the gift of communicating with spirit. Whether, a medium does it, or you try it for yourself -automatic trance writing has always brought much peace, happiness, closure and guidance to all of my clients. The written word can be life changing!

Gina Cannone

INTRODUCTION

To begin, I believe we all have the ability to tap into the higher source of knowledge for connection with spirit, guidance for a better life and for peace and closure. For those who prefer to experience speaking with spirit with a professional medium, this book will enlighten you on what automatic writing is and how it works first hand from my own sessions. For the readers who want to learn how to actually practice this, you will get an enormous amount of information on how-to properly and safely communicate with spirit through automatic trance writing.

Automatic writing is an alleged psychic ability allowing a person to produce written words without consciously writing. The words are claimed to arise from a *subconscious, spiritual or supernatural source.*

WIKIPEDIA

Automatic writing can occur through a trance state within and from the subconscious or by a spirit controlling the movement of the writer. I automatic trance write through my subconscious. I speak with spirit and convey the messages verbally along with writing whatever comes from mind to hand. Being a board certified advanced clinical hypnotherapist, I have the ability to enter trance quite easily and effortlessly. I enter this relaxed-meditative-hypnotic state and open myself up to the spirit world, asking for only those loved ones connected with whom I am reading to come forth and give messages. What I ask for is details that they would only know and connect with, along with any messages they want to send. I am in a trance state and my hand effortlessly flows across the pages doodling out sentences, pictures, letters and numbers. I'm always amazed to see what transpires on paper and the client is usually moved and teary-eyed. I allow great detail to come forth and my gift is authentic, truthful and successful.

The practice of automatic trance writing can bring out messages and information that otherwise may have never been brought out. Sometimes warning messages are sent that help heal or direct someone to heed caution. It is a wonderful modality to have these messages in writing for keepsake.

It is believed that automatic writing is a form of telepathy. But, even if so, other information that the client wasn't even thinking about comes through. Information that they have to recall and think about what the writings are trying to convey. The process when experienced by an authentic medium is none the less amazing, baffling, enlightening and memorable.

Automatic writing isn't something to dabble in for fun. You are opening yourself up to the spirit world and learning how to open and close a session safely and properly is a must. When I am out with friends or at a party, people will ask me to read them. I always say that I could, but prefer to do it the proper way; which includes a calm quiet place, a white candle and an opening prayer. Then add they can make an appointment. Beginner beware…do not practice openly, not even for fun or a test. Forces beyond your control are around and you must be aware of the dangers of doing this.

Within this book you will learn about the "trance" experience, how to enter that state and to trust the messages from the subconscious level. Learning also how to open and close properly and respecting the spirit world.

Exercises to practice this form of divination and to decipher your symbols that flow through.
It will take time and practice to be able to analyze what you have written and have a handle on it.

I will include many samples of my automatic trance writings from actual sessions with clients. I will explain how the messages were deciphered and explained to the client.
I am an artist and a pianist, but I find it funny that I cannot draw so well when in trance, but good enough to relay the message. This is one way I absolutely know that I am in trance, for if I were consciously aware I would be able to draw perfectly.

Communicating with the spirit world through automatic writing is a form of mediumship. Allowing spirit to communicate message through your subconscious when in a trance state or deep meditative state. In rare cases, sometimes spirit will actually move your hand. Words, sentences, pictures, letters and numbers quickly appear. The writings can sometimes be very neat and clear or sloppily written. I call it mind scrapping. There are no paragraphs, punctuation marks or reasonable order to the writings. Putting the pieces together and asking the client continuously if the writings have meaning to them is what keeps you on track and connected with spirit.

Respecting the "spirits" you are contacting and having a "rapport" with them is crucial to the success of a session. I am always thankful and appreciative that they came through. This is not a game and people need and want to hear from loved ones that have passed, so utmost respect is first and foremost.

Whether, you are just interested in this form of mediumship or want to learn and practice it for yourself,
you will learn from this book what you need to embrace the other side. Understanding the messages, learning how to enter trance, trusting your images and thoughts and letting it flow onto paper. Opening a new world to communicate and to also get guidance.

Awakening your spirituality and intuitiveness will allow you to experience contact and communication with spirit and to enjoy knowing that they do watch over and help guide us through life. Automatic trance writing is beneficial for many reasons; to connect with the other side and loved ones who have passed, to get guidance for our own personal life, to receive messages for others as a medium, and to believe and know spirit is with us always.

I truly believe it is a blessing that I can communicate with spirit. I am ecstatic to be able to give messages to those who really want to hear from their deceased loved ones and help them heal and understand that they are still with us.

Embrace and enjoy reading and learning about the wonderful world of writing messages from beyond.

*"Death in the physical is the birth in the spiritual.
Birth in the physical is death in the spiritual"*

EDGAR CAYCE

TABLE OF CONTENTS

CHAPTER 1

WHAT IS AUTOMATIC *"TRANCE"* WRITING

"Trance" writing is the process of being in a deep trance state or hypnotic state, then writing or doodling images, words, sentences, numbers and letters, unaware of what the outcome is until out of the trance state. This is done with eyes closed; relaxed with pen in hand letting the subconscious thoughts emerge through the hand. You also can enter a light trance, and allow spirit to send you messages to your mind, then for you to write what you see or hear.

I as a medium and a board certified clinical hypnotherapist, enter easily into a light trance state upon beginning all my reading sessions with clients. I open and close my eyes during the session and allow my hand to just write whatever comes from spirit. I consider myself in a light trance and am able to talk in between the writing. Spirit communicates with me by forming messages in my mind. I experience "visions" during the trance state and they seem to effortlessly appear on paper. I hear words, see symbols, signs and then write and scribble away. Sentences do come through-but NOT in my words, but the words the spirit is speaking. I write exactly what I hear or see, never changing it.

I ask for details, more information, and the names or initials of the spirit. I want as much detail as possible from spirit and I am always thankful for them speaking with me.

My psychic "clair" gifts along with the automatic trance writings has brought about some of the most intriguing messages. These psychic gifts are also stronger and clearer during the automatic writing process. The outcomes of my sessions contain unbelievable messages and information I could never know. These written messages are undeniably from spirit and/or a higher source. Most of my clients sit in awe, mouth-opened, teary-eyed and astonished. The messages have no meaning for me-they are messages for them and only them. Upon finishing and hearing what the client confirms and says afterwards stills amazes me. I feel truly blessed to be able to give to others the connection of spirit.

Spirit communication through automatic writing requires some practice. Shutting your conscious mind off and letting your subconscious mind move to the forefront allowing a freedom of thoughts and images to enter. Just letting go and not to think about what you are experiencing, hearing, seeing or writing. Once you begin to think about what is happening your conscious mind is waking up, remaining in that trance state, deep meditative place is where automatic writing is authentic. The words and sentences are the spirits words and will not sound like the way you would say something, for it's not you. This can be frightening at first to a novice and to never be dabbled in again, or the fear will pass, exhilaration takes over and a spiritual spark to learn more is awakened.

My automatic trance writing begins with a shift of the minds, a prayer and lighting of a white candle. Then I allow my conscious mind to move to the back or resting place, while the subconscious moves to the front. This is self-hypnosis and you are aware of what is going on around you and with the person you are reading. I am personally not in full trance, but a light trance. I ask that *only the loved ones* of whom I am reading come through with messages specifically for them. The messages are astonishingly correct and filled with extreme details only the client would know. I too am amazed after each session, since I do not know what will be spoken to me and appear on the paper until in the process. Also, only understanding all that I have written after the client explains to me what it all means.

I believe this is a safe and easy form of communicating with spirit. Each medium or individual that practices automatic writing will develop their own style and unique system. Images, signs and symbols mean things and with practice you can understand what they mean for you to translate. An example of this are some of my symbols, such as; when spirit arm is down, showing me holding hands with a child- means; a baby/child has passed, whether from a miscarriage, abortion or actually death after birth. Another example is when I ask what they have died from; spirit will tap on the location of the body to show me what caused their death. I will discuss these signs and symbols along with examples of my writings in another chapter. But, with practice you will eventually be able to decipher and understand what is being sent to you. With automatic writing you can get visions of how and where spirit has passed. There is a sense that Spirit wants to be heard and connected, not wanting to leave sometimes.

During an automatic writing session, I move in and out of different states of awareness. Opening and closing my eyes, putting my hands over my face, listening to spirit and allowing the messages in. I feel detached from myself, communicating with spirit for the sole purpose of retrieving messages for the person I am reading. I can also feel emotion (clairsentience) from spirit and pass that information along as well during the writing process.

Since I am clairvoyant (clear seeing-see future), the last part of my reading & automatic writing sessions concludes with information for their personal life, future and any issues needing clarification. I also ask prior if they want to know the good and the not so good, getting permission to give that information I receive. At some point, questions are allowed to be asked, the automatic writing continues and answers come forth.

My clients are usually in shock, teary-eyed and feel an enormous connection was made from their loved ones. They take peace and comfort with them; along with an experience to remember and the actual automatic writing papers to enjoy again and again.

We all do some form of automatic writing on a daily basis. Doodling while on the phone. Scribbling when on a skype call or internet conference. We are not concentrating on the actual doodling or scribbling, the subconscious is writing and the conscious mind is focused on the call. That is automatic writing.

Automatic writing is the simplest and easiest form of communication for novices. The writing of words, phrases, letters, numbers and pictures arise from a subconscious, spiritual or supernatural source and is a great way to experience spirit communication. It is not too scary and can be an amazing enlightening experience.

When I do my writing during a reading session, it is intertwined with my other psychic abilities; clairvoyance (clear seeing), clairalience (clear smelling), and clairaudience (clear hearing). As a medium, everything is working and I use all my psychic senses. When in a light trance, I'm moving in and out, writing then talking, back to writing.

Some of you may be psychic and just want to learn more on how to automatic write, and some of you may just want to experience or communicate with spirit for your own guidance- automatic writing is a wonderful tool. It is a great way to access your deceased loved ones and spirit guides whenever and wherever you want. Knowing you are capable of connecting when you need guidance, advice, and direction.

When doing automatic writing, I find that sometimes I have to ask the client to help piecing the words, pictures together and connecting the images to the spirit that is communicating. Meaning, when I first start a reading and open up, many spirits come through for the client. I immediately start to get little bits and pieces from each of them and then have to know who and what is from which spirit. If you are doing this for oneself - you'll know what all the writings mean.

I have wonderful automatic writing stories from a psychic workshop I was giving. The class was paired off and could write for themselves or for the other person. I was teaching the automatic writing process and instructed everyone to listen to my voice, meditate, and to keep eyes closed or open and begin writing. Allowing the hand to freely move across the paper. To WRITE whatever comes to mind, to not think but, allow it to happen. Some hands were moving very slowly, some quickly, some drew pictures, others, full sentences.

When I ended the practice session, I asked each group to go over what they wrote and experienced.

One person seemed upset and I asked her to share her experience. She said she didn't get anything and her paper doodle didn't mean anything to her. I asked, "what did you draw?"

She answered, "It's dumb, I don't want to say." I said that nothing was dumb and it always means something to someone, so what is it? She said, "a bumble bee-I just see bumble bees." The girl next to her starts crying and says my dog just passed away and we dressed him for Halloween as a bumble bee.

Another person wrote in Spanish and he didn't even speak a word of it. The message was for his wife.

Automatic Writing is a great way to begin your psychic path. It's enlightening, fun, and comfortable. With practice a beginner can communicate with deceased loved ones and then ask for advice for themselves or for others. It's one the easiest types of psychic communication to develop. I'm sure there is some skepticism when reading about automatic writing, but, beware and be careful, it works and you must not just open yourself up and start writing without the proper opening and closing. When I begin a reading session, I always open properly with prayer and then in the closing I thank spirit and shut it off before the next reading. You can type on computer or hand write, but most people prefer to hand-write, as I do.

Over time and with practice, you can build your trust, decipher your messages, and easily communicate with spirit. Allowing your inner guidance, your higher self, to help create or guide the messages you write.

CHAPTER 2

THERE IS A PURPOSE

What is the purpose of automatic writing? What is the purpose of speaking to spirit?

There are many reasons why we would want to speak with spirit;

- Inner peace and clarity
- Closure
- Heal from grief
- Release any Guilt
- Need answers

There are also many reasons why spirit would want to communicate with us;

- Bring us happiness and peace
- Send messages
- Give guidance for your life
- Heed warnings for protection
- Let you know they ARE watching over and there to help you

The reason I wanted to write about automatic writing is that it is easy and comfortable for anyone to try. I also have much success with my readings by doing automatic writing along with my other psychic abilities. You need to be in a quiet space, and open to hearing, seeing, smelling and feeling. Spirit will come through in any or all of these senses.

There are two ways to actually try automatic writing. One is to go into trance, with eyes closed, just allow the message to flow through your hand, through the subconscious level. You will not know what was written until you come out of trance and review your writings. The second way is to be in a light trance, but with eyes open, writing what you hear, see, smell and feel. For beginners I recommend the first technique to adjust to your inner senses and guides.

We have all experienced moments in life when we may have felt an unknown force guide us, direct us, protect us and even speak to us. You may have experienced spirit coming to you through dreams, or when bathing or floating in water. Their purpose is to tell you something, get you a message, help you get on or stay on the right path.

When I am giving a reading and doing automatic writing, I see images in my head (clairvoyance), I hear sounds and voices (clairaudience), I sometimes can smell something related to that spirit (clairalience) or feel the essence of the spirit (clairsentience). Spirit guides, Angels, deceased loved ones come to us in many different ways. You will receive messages; just open yourself to listening to your body, mind and spirit.

I speak to GOD, my Angels, Spirit Guides (deceased loved ones). When just needing to make something happen in life, finding loving relationships, career changes, guidance on issues such as; moving, divorcing, starting new businesses, etc. I would then speak to my spirit guides. If I feel I need a blessing or miracle, I speak to GOD and my

Angels. If I have fear or need protection, I speak to my Angels and Spirit Guides. I also, light a candle, play relaxing background music, and say an opening and closing prayer. I am always thankful and appreciative for their assistance. I ONLY ask for specific spirits to help. I do not at all open the doorway to just any spirit. This can cause you much trouble. Positive thoughts at all times, remaining bonded with GOD and Angels.

GOD, Angels and Spirit Guides are there to protect, guide, warn, and send what you need for your life's purpose. It's an extraordinary tool to have and use.

CHAKRA 6 is your third eye, located in the center of your forehead. The third eye sees into your soul, as well as seeing into the psychic and spiritual realms. Keeping yourself positive and clear is important when using your third eye. Opening and closing it properly is essential to clearing oneself after each communication session. You must safely navigate through these spiritual realms. Take great care to protect yourself and the third eye with spiritually protective and positive forces.

AJNA, or third-eye chakra, is the sixth primary chakra in the body according to Hindu tradition. It is a part of the brain which can be made more powerful through repetition, like a muscle, and it signifies the conscience. While a person's two eyes sees the real world, the third eye is believed to reveal insights about the future. The third eye chakra connects people to their intuitions, gives them the ability to communicate with the world, and helps them receive messages from the past and the future.

WIKIPEDIA

The purpose for a medium, as I am, to automatic write, is to help others heal, communicate with their loved ones, and to give them something tangible to review and experience the reading session whenever they want. Also, to show the writings to others and enjoy the enlightening experiencing again and again.

How terrible it must be for Angels and Spirit Guides to NOT be called upon. They are around for us to ask and receive, rely on for guidance, bringing us freedom and peace to journey our true "purposeful" path in life. So many need to learn that they can rely on their Spiritual sources. I am beyond grateful to have reached a time in my life that I only rely on them. My inner guidance, my spiritual guidance, my Angels and GOD has not ever failed me. My psychic abilities are a blessing. I use them to help and heal others and to guide my own life.

 I really can't imagine going through life and not communicating with spirit. I want everyone to experience this wonderful connection. Automatic trance writing is an amazing technique that you can try for yourself and see what happens.

There is a purpose for prayer, for speaking to higher powers for help, guidance and answers. To be able to let go of limiting beliefs, step out of your comfort zone, reach for your goals and dreams is a great reason to speak to the other side. To be guided and sent all you need is enough purpose for me to connect with spirit. When your intentions are true, from the soul, you ask and you will receive. Whether you hear it within you, write it through trance writings, or just feel the right way to turn…they are with you pushing you and steering you. Listen to your own inner voice for they speak to your very soul.

ANGELS serve as GOD'S messengers to mankind. Angels play a very important role; to assist, protect and defend. Also, to console those who need comforting through great suffering. It is written that we come with our own personal Angel (guardians). The purpose of this is to help guide and protect us here on earth, so that we can enter heaven. It's believed that when we face a critical junction in our life, an Angel's purpose is to help us find a smoother path and guide us through the challenges we have to bear.

Angel's have spoken to me many times. I moved three times because of hearing an Angel's voice telling me to. I wrote my first book and this one also because I heard an Angel voice telling me to write. I still had the choice of not listening, but my life would not be as it is today. I always listen and I am always grateful afterwards.

If you believe in ANGELS and Spirit Guides, a higher power, GOD, then you believe they can hear you. You can talk to them- ask them for anything you need. Use your own intuitions to communicate with them and your life will change.

Purpose of Archangels-SPEAK to them for the following:

- **Archangel Raphael:** *"Healing Power of God"* - Brings healing to humans and animals. Call upon him to assist, heal and to protect you.

- **Archangel Gabriel:** *"Strength from God"*- known as the "Messenger Angel" and communicator. For mediums and psychics, ask Gabriel to help you receive clear messages.

- **Archangel Ariel:** *"Lion of God"* – protects and heals things living in nature; animals, fish, birds, Call upon Ariel for healing of any pets.

- **Archangel Michael:** *"He Who Is Like God"* – Turn to Michael if need help and guidance for career and life aspirations. You can receive courage to accomplish your goals and grow spiritually and emotionally. For powerful protection against all negativity.

- **Archangel Chamuel:** *"He Who Sees or Seeks God"* – the archangel of love, peaceful and loving relationships. When your relationships need help, speak to Chamuel to give you strength to end or begin a relationship. Also, there to help those who hearts are blocked; depressed, despair and hopelessness... (broken-hearted).

- **Archangel Uriel:** *"God is Light"* – helps you find inner truth and light and to embrace inner wisdom. For those who may be feeling "stuck" and need to guidance to move forward, ask Uriel for help and your life will turn more to the positive, and protected from the negative.

So, if and when you decide to do your first automatic writing session, decide on a few questions you need answers to, call upon the Archangel that may help you most, and begin your trance. You may be very surprised on what ends up on your paper. If not clear at first, not to worry, practice is required for clarity.

I sat one night thinking of my relationships. I have had a broken heart for years, and many blockers keep me from being in a relationship. So I enter a light a trance and started typing and asking questions to Archangel Chamuel to send me a message. This is what I typed...

There s a way to find him open your heart to the light   I will send very soon no yes yes work first   on way on way o you   dddddddddo believe again long distance he will come   you will know ...

Smile if you are true...full I understand soon soon
10/12/16

Everyone has a reason – a purpose to call upon the Angels and Spirit guides. We all need guidance and inner wisdom to make wise choices. The real purpose to communicate is to allow yourself to hear and listen to the messages, so that you can direct and create the life you want. Become a better person. To receive answers to questions that help you move on. To heal. To eliminate doubt. For courage, strength, motivation and energy. Whether for yourself or for others, communicating with spirit is one of the most powerful tools you can use, so why not.

CHAPTER 3

THE "TRANCE" EXPERIENCE

So what is a "trance" state of mind? The term trance is usually associated with hypnosis, meditation, magic and prayer. We naturally go into trance state every night when trying to fall asleep. The space between not fully aware of what is going on around you, but not asleep is the trance state. When in trance, your focused within and seem to be disconnected to the outer world, but still aware. While in this hypnotic trance state you experience a heightened sense of awareness with an intense focus of inward attention. You are NOT asleep when in trance. As a board certified clinical hypnotherapist, speaker and instructor, I apply the techniques discussed in this chapter that work for me and will help you achieve the "trance" state when beginning a spiritual automatic writing session.

Breathing techniques and relaxation techniques are used when trying to enter a deep relaxed state, or trance state.

- Visualizing – imagine a peaceful tranquil place that you know relaxes you.
- Eye Fixation – focus on a spot and relax, breathe and clear the mind of thoughts and distractions.

The more you practice this the easier it gets. I enter that zone fairly easily and usually after a few deep breaths and a prayer, I'm in deep focus and ready to read and automatic write for my client. This is self-hypnosis and you may have to try a few different techniques to find what is most comfortable and works best for you.

The funny part about being in a trance state is that you are so focused inward, but can be still aware of everything around you. In a deep trance state, you may not hear or care about anything that is going on around you. We all do this naturally and a few examples of this is;

- When watching a movie and totally engrossed - not hearing someone call you.
- When driving on the highway late at night – and suddenly you're at your exit without knowing it.
- When reading a book – passage of time is distorted.

The depth of a hypnotic trance can vary from very light to extremely deep. When automatic writing, I am in a *very light trance*. I prefer to be in a light trance allowing me to talk to my clients at the same time. I seem to keep my eyes closed during the inward focus on spirit communication, then opening them to write and deliver messages to client. I also tend to look off into the corner- not looking at the client-which keeps me in "trance" state and focused. This trance state is extremely beneficial in clearing the mind to allow the psychic "clairs" to open and work at their best capacity.

Those who practice meditation, hypnosis, and prayer-which is most of us…understand the inner focus. It's important to achieve this state prior to trying an automatic writing session and communicating with spirit so that you are receptive and open to the messages. A clear channel is needed for accessing truthful messages.

Giving readings everyday speeds up the process. The relaxation techniques and self-hypnosis allows me to enter trance and receive messages from the loved ones of my clients. I write exactly what I hear, see, feel-never altering the words or images. From this trance state, authentic truthfulness comes forth.

Hypnosis; the trance state, is brought about by shifting the balance between two different parts of the mind. The conscious mind moves to the back and becomes passive, while the sub-conscious move to the front becoming accessible. This state of trance allows you; to be open, to focus inward, to access your inner guidance, access spiritual guidance, hear messages, and helps in all areas of your life, where you need direction, assistance, or motivation.

The trance state is not a sleep state. It is the day-dreamy state of mind often experienced by people who meditate, listen to music or undergo a hypnotic induction. It is a very relaxing and enjoyable state to be in.
The new world of spiritualism believes you can tap into the subconscious mind to write whatever comes to mind. Opening and closing properly is important. This is not a game. Respecting spirit and asking only those loved ones that have passed, angels or higher divine source, to come forth.

There have been numerous famous psychics that have practiced automatic writing. People such as; Jane Roberts, Helene Smith, Helen Schucman, Lenora Piper-other famous mediums we know today; John Edwards, Allison DuBois. All worth examining and reading about.

As a medium, I connect and communicate with spirit when giving a reading. I use automatic writing as an additive tool. More messages seem to come through when doodling on paper. Since I am in a light trance state when giving a reading, I seldom remember afterwards what I wrote or said. If we are taught to pray to our loved ones and angels and they can hear us; then I believe we all can communicate with them. My clients always state after their reading, that the reading and automatic writing was wonderful and amazing, and truly enlightening. They seem to be more at ease and peaceful afterwards too. I get a lot of hugs.

When in a trance, you may hear, see or feel, messages coming through from spirit guides, angels or the divine power. You freely let yourself write whatever comes to mind and then review afterwards. Trance opens and enters the subconscious mind-you may predict something, get answers to questions, get closure, and overall feel enlightened and exhilarated!

The "trance" state can easily be achieved through self-hypnosis. Relaxation and breathing techniques help get you into trance. An easy way to warm up to this art of communication is to have a pen and paper handy when talking on the phone. Take a few deep breaths, relax and begin your conversation. Then pick up the pen and allow yourself to doodle while continuing your conversation. Pay no attention your pen. Letting your hand doodle whatever it wants to. Most of us do this naturally. This will help you to practice talking to someone while doodling random thoughts from the subconscious. You can then write a question down first, then begin your phone call-see what happens…Remember to always say a prayer to open to spirit world. If a session feels negative, immediately close the session. I have yet to have a negative session, my prayers are strong, appreciative with unwavering faith.

The process of opening is extremely important. The outline for this is:

- Get comfortable in chair with legs uncrossed.
- Take three deep breaths-in through the nose-out through the mouth. Inhaling slowing and slowing your breathing down.
- Visualize a stairway going down to your inner core.
- Count to ten -with each count go down the stairs saying going deeper-going deeper.
- Get focused within.
- Say a *prayer* asking that only those loved ones for yourself or other person are allowed through to give messages. Keep the white light around for protection during the session.
- State why you are calling upon them. Need assistance, guidance, answer to a question.
- Then visualize your third eye opening, allowing to SEE images.
- Then visualize a zipper on top of your head opening, allowing to HEAR messages.
- Ask for details. Ask for names, letters, to show how they passed.
- Use ALL your senses to receive information. See, Hear, Feel, Smell.
- Begin WRITING everything that is coming through. Do not eliminate anything. Everything is important. Do NOT think about what you are receiving, just allow the thoughts to come and write-write-write.
- Give yourself half hour or so and then end session.
- CLOSE properly. Thank spirit for coming, close your zipper on top of head, close your third eye and end session. It's important to close so that you do not carry spirit with you all day.
- Evaluate what was written.

As I spoke of earlier, I write during my reading sessions and talk while writing; asking if the symbols, letters, numbers and words mean anything and connecting the writings to the spirits coming forth. At first, you may not understand all the information and the way it is coming through. This takes practice and time. Each Psychic Medium has their own symbols and ways messages are received. It's a learning process. My symbol for that a child has passed is shown to me by the arm being down-holding hands with a child. This is what I see, and how I decipher it. I will talk more about deciphering messages within the book.

Practical advice before starting automatic writing. If you already meditate or do self-hypnosis, then jumping right in is fine. For those who need to learn how to focus inward and to just concentrate on inner awareness; then I suggest you practice meditating and entering a light trance state a few times first.

There are many things that can block you from experiencing communication.

- Being too tired, too busy or stressed slows down your vibration.
- Alcohol/drugs diminish proper communication. Psychic exercises should NOT be done if you have been drinking or doing any form of drugs. You risk attracting undesirable spirits. If you have a drinking or drug issue you should not be doing this at all.
- We don't know how to connect with spirit.
- We doubt if we really can connect.
- Looking for a different answer.
- Not grounded/not properly prepared for opening
- Too focused on the conscious (rational) mind instead of the subconscious level.

- Not listening to your inner voice-your inner intuition.
- Thinking, over thinking, fear of being wrong all get in the way of receiving accurate and important messages.
- Avoid practicing in bad weather-it can make you can feel unbalanced or distracted.

Practice this with yourself first. If wanting to practice with others, then work with those you trust.

CHAPTER 4

WHY WRITE?

Automatic trance writing is one of the easiest ways to communicate with spirit. It can be done by anyone, anywhere and at any time. Psychic Mediums, as myself use a variety of techniques to increase vibration, spiritual connection, and to receive truthful messages. The technique of automatic writing allows you to communicate on your own, without the need of a Psychic Medium. Allowing you to get access to guidance, closure, answers, and anything else you may need from speaking to your Angels and Spirit guides.

I write for many reasons. It is part of my work as a Psychic Medium. It helps me to reach higher and stronger vibrations. The writing within my readings are detailed, clear messages and come in quite strong when I have pen in hand. Since I am an artist, drawing pictures appear quite easily, along with words, sentences, numbers and letters. It is a technique that enhances my psychic "clairs" during my readings. The "clairs" that I happen to be extremely strong in are;

- CLAIRVOYANT-clear seeing, usually comes through as mini pictures, sometime a flash of a scene, just seeing images crossing over the mind.

Full movie-like images in dreams, and SEEING the images in color also. Strong visual pictures.

- CLAIRALIENCE-clear smelling, acquiring knowledge when smells come through. Often smelling flowers, perfume, food, smoke, or anything else related to the spirit that is sending information by scent. Sometimes, others around you can smell spirit also.

- CLAIRAUDIENCE-clear hearing, allows you to hear voices, sounds, music and tones within your inner mental ear. Usually only you can hear this.

- CLAIRSENTIENCE-clear feeling or touching, feeling the vibrations and emotions, of humans, of spirit and of animals. Feeling these emotions can be overwhelming and should be controlled. Also, feeling spirit physically touching a part of you.

All the above "clairs" are my strongest. During my readings, I open up all my psychic "clair" senses, allowing them to be fully accessible by spirit. The automatic writing allows me to write all that I SEE, SMELL, HEAR and FEEL.

I have seen full visual images of accidents, deaths, births, etc. - from the good to the not so good. I can see illness also. I have smelled a variety of scents always correlating to the spirit that is present. I've heard many messages that have been a great guidance to my life journey and with helping others for what they need for their life.

Most people who are interested in the spiritual world are usually curious about the methods one can use to receive information. Trying these different methods to communicate and access knowledge. Tarot cards, crystal balls, scrying mirrors, are all different modalities to practice.

Automatic writing method is quite amazing. You can keep your eyes closed and go into trance and just let spirit move your hand. Have a question or two ready before you start. You will not know what you are writing until you open your eyes and see what is on paper. This is one way to automatic write. The other is to be in a light trance, as I do, and be able to talk and write what is coming through my psychic "clairs". I see what I am drawing and writing and speak throughout my readings. If I am alone and want to automatic write for myself, I will keep eyes closed and see what happens. Both ways are absolutely amazing and enlightening.

I write, because interesting enough, my psychic abilities are stronger, clearer, and it is relaxing for me. Automatic writing also helps the client who is watching it all appear on paper. They get to experience the full essence of spirit coming through in multiple ways. They see the writing appearing effortlessly, the sentences or words may be exactly what their loved ones would say, they get to evaluate the messages and pictures visually, helping them to connect the pieces.

Why write? You may want to automatic write for many reasons.

1. You may just want to experience it and see what happens.

2. You may feel safer doing this method, being too afraid to try other methods.
3. You can access your higher self and get answers to questions for your life.
4. You may not be clairvoyant or clairaudient to full capacity.
5. You want to connect with spirit and this is the easiest method.

Usually a skilled medium is recommended for all divination methods. If you are unsure and not ready to try yourself, seek a highly skilled Psychic Medium. Letting entities from other planes of existence in, allowing the messages to come forth through you and automatic writing is not a game. I want everyone to experience the wonderment of it all, but to be careful, thoughtful, and open and close with prayer. When automatic writing, there is no punctuations, capitalization, and if channeled, no pictures, just sentences will appear. Automatic writing can be enlightening and amazing, but also scary. Just keep in mind that you are opening yourself to the spirit world when practicing this.

You should have a reason why you want to write. Have your questions ready and then begin your opening prayer before allowing yourself to write or type. Please time yourself and end the session when time is up. End with a closing prayer, thanking your spirit guides for coming through and assisting you with what you needed.

Even after all the psychic readings and automatic writings I have done, I am still to this day amazed at what happens and appears. My clients are also totally amazed and leave with a feeling of peace, hope, and happiness knowing they are watched and looked after by their spirit guides and angels.

I want everyone to know that I was brought up a strict Catholic and I have fought within myself to do what is right. There are mixed thoughts about psychics and mediums, the methods they use and the outcomes. My first and foremost tool I use is the power of prayer to connect with (God) the higher power, angels and spirit guides. My psychic abilities are a gift, being a medium is a gift, and I always respect it and access them from the same place of higher power, guidance and goodness. Automatic writing when respected and done properly, is something amazing to experience.

You should ONLY automatic write if your intentions are good, respectful and need assistance and guidance. Have a reason to communicate with spirit and have questions ready in mind. Practice a little each day and let yourself be open to whatever comes, writing the words without judgment or expectation. Remember, the words should flow through you, from the divine, from your psychic abilities and not from the conscious mind.

I am so thankful that I am gifted and automatic write for my clients. I usually have four pages of words, letters, numbers, pictures and sentences for them to keep. I am just as amazed with the outcomes of automatic writing as my clients. The information is always validated, and brings enormous peace, closure, spiritual growth and connection to their deceased loved ones. Obtaining details that the client would only know, is essential for me as a Psychic Medium.

CHAPTER 5

AUTOMATIC WRITINGS FROM MY SESSIONS

This chapter contains numerous automatic writings from my reading sessions. I photograph most of them and then give them to my clients when their reading is over. My out-of-town clients that do skype readings get a photograph and I keep the original. You'll see a pattern in how my writings come about. Everyone has their own style, their own way of auto writing.

I always start with how many females and males are present and who they are; Mother, Father, Grandparents, Husband, Wife, etc. I then get information on how they passed and continue to get *details*. It builds as I go along and I confirm with client the information coming through. It comes through in words, sentences, pictures, letters and numbers. I use all my psychic "clairs" and mediumship during the session. I always begin with the mediumship of communicating with spirit and then end with the psychic "clair" reading. Automatic writing the entire time. It helps to establish a system, your own style, to receive these messages. Asking for specific details that only the client would know what it means. This is the miracle of automatic writing. Enlightening to both the psychic writer and the client every time!

The writings usually come through in pieces, and is put together like a puzzle. I speak while doing automatic writing, saying what I am seeing and hearing and transfering it all onto paper. I ask the client if it has meaning to them so that I know I am connecting properly and always validating the reading.

My clients are truly amazed and love the experience, resulting in many referrals. Skeptics that come to see me are absolutely enlightened and bewildered by my sessions. They experience a spiritual connection that is unique to them, often leaving a believer and wanting to come back for another session.

Every Pyschic Medium who automatic writes has their own set of unique symbols and techniques. Learning how the messages are being sent through via symbols or signs, need to be deciphered.

For example;
- When spirit shows me their arm down as if holding hands with a child, this is how I interpret that a child has passed. Could of passed by miscarriage, abortion, or actual death after birth.
- Two fists hitting each other means; sudden impact, death on impact.
- An empty hand held out means; there for the passing.

This takes time to understand, but once you get it, the spiritual world opens up.

52

Automatic "Trance" Writing # 1

This session was evaluated and proven correct by client. Her Aunt who was her second mom, was murdered, but deemed an accident-that is why murder and accident was written. The body was never found, hence; writing the words NO "Body".

I also wrote, that there was a male who died in a car accident from a head injury.

The words shocking and On News, was confirmed that all of this was on the News.

The picture of the cross with doodling around it – was spirit showing me a cross tattoo with names of loved ones around it. She showed me the tattoo after the reading which was exactly what I drew.

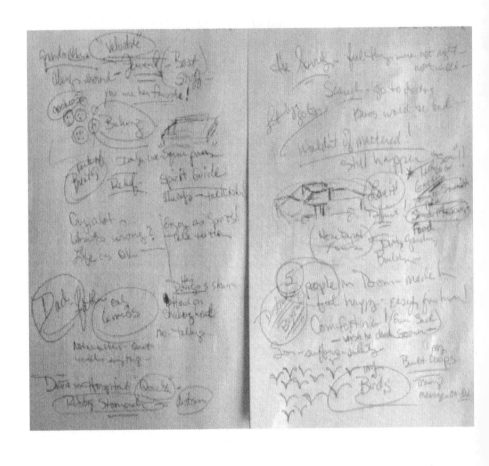

Automatic "Trance" Writing # 2

This reading started out with the grandmother coming
through. Bringing up her jewelry and baking. A detail
written that she only used square pans for cakes, never
round made the client laugh. Confirming that she only used
square pans.

Further along, her Dad came through saying he died quick
and in hospital. On next page, the Father mentioned his
birds and I drew lots of birds, but then I wrote- built my
coops. The client by now has tears in her eyes, confirming
his pigeons and coops.

Automatic "Trance" Writing # 3

This reading looks messy, but to the client it was absolutely spot on. The deceased grandmother showed me a diamond ring that was given to the client. Also, I drew a fleur-de-lis tattoo with a name below. The client started crying stating she had a fleur-de-lis tattoo with the name on it. The plane signifies a trip, and I wrote 10 days. That was how long her trip was planned for.

58

Automatic "Trance" Writing # 4

This session was incredible. Father had died-Baseball fan-number 9 was his number-he had many bird feeders and said "just feed them".   Then a young male came through and said it was an accident-but so sorry for destroying family. Bottom left you see I wrote choked on t-up (throw-up). This person showed me what happened at his passing, and I felt very sick during this part of the reading. It was confirmed that his friend was not feeling well, laid down on couch, then died due to choking on his throw-up.

Some deaths that I see clairvoyantly, are disturbing. It takes time to grasp control emotionally on this.
The vision is like a mini-movie. I tell what I am seeing and then write the notes.

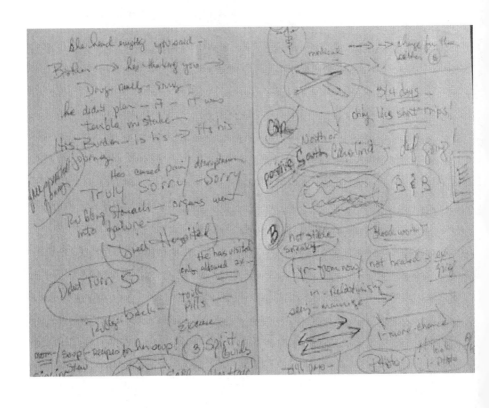

Automatic "Trance" Writing # 5

This session seemed to be a suicide, but it is stated from spirit that it was an accident. He was 49, hence writing didn't turn 50. Organ failure, took pills, sorry -all messages sent.
Trip to South Carolina, looking for 2nd home by water.
Client confirmed all.

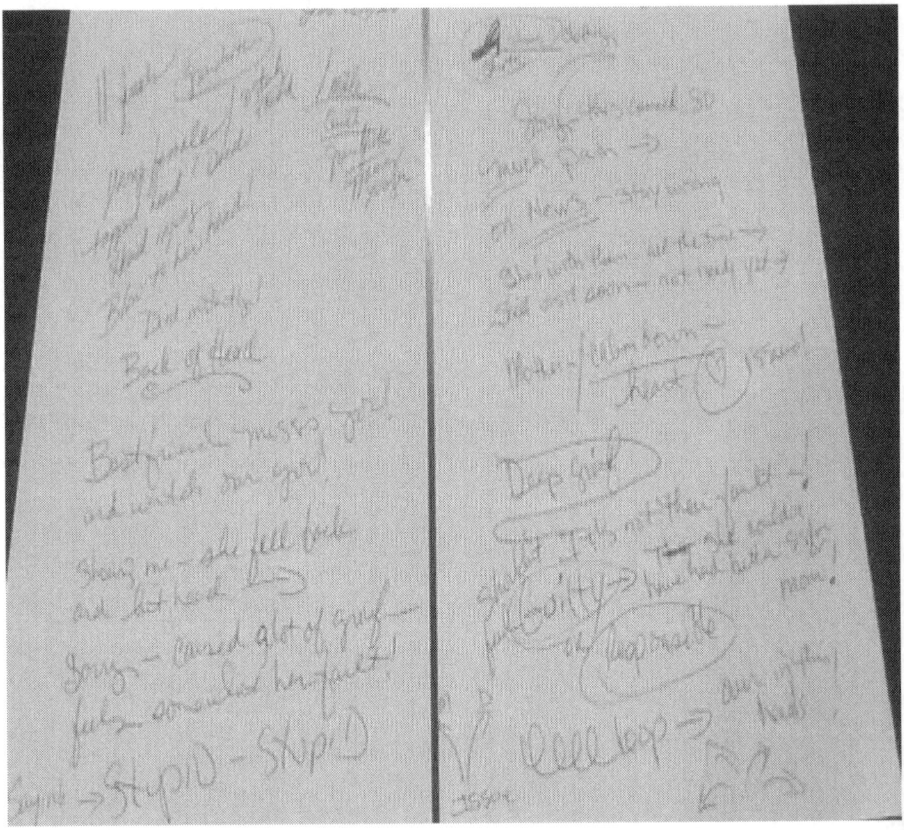
Back of Hand
Best friend misses girl
STUPID - STUPID
on News
Deep grief
Responsible
ISSUE

Automatic "Trance" Writing # 6

A young female came through and tapped her head and said she died instantly -back of head. Saying it was somewhat her fault-Stupid-stupid…
I also wrote -On News- story wrong…

All of the above writings were validated by my clients. Most cry or become teary-eyed when the words start to appear. They cannot believe what comes out and how much detail is sent from spirit. The messages are for them, so I do not filter anything, I just write what my psychic abilities are receiving.

I am frequently asked what I see, how do I hear these messages. I am psychically strong in most of the *"Clairs"*, but the two that are the strongest is what helps when communicating.

I am *clairvoyant*, so I see images. I can see spirit in light form most of the time. Then they show me things about them. They may show me hats, numbers, their initials etc. anything that pertains to them and who they were. Sometimes it is like a mini-movie.

I am also *clairaudient*, so I hear sounds, voices, music. My inner ear can just hear faint sounds that I understand and transfer them into words on paper.

It is quite amazing to automatic write, and I enjoy giving the gift of connection.

CHAPTER 6

DECIPHERING THE WRITINGS

When you decide to start practicing automatic writing, you may get frustrated and/or confused by what you are writing. I recommend you write everything you hear, feel, see, smell, taste. Leave nothing out. Anything and everything that comes to mind is to be put down on paper. Even if you think it is crazy, stupid, funny-doesn't matter what you think-the messages have meaning.

Early in my spiritual career, I was afraid to write and say everything I was receiving. Some things were not so nice, like the session I had about the choking on throw-up. Over time, you realize that you MUST write exactly what is being sent.

Messages from beyond can be literal or symbolic. All kinds of messages can come through; things to accomplish, life's purposes, people to watch over, advice and guidance for your life direction, symbols that have meaning, apologies, songs, poetry and more. Always trust your own interpretation and see the patterns in which they come in.

Some of my symbols from Spirit:

- **Open empty hand held out**-there for the passing and thank you. Usually hand was held at death.
- **Arm down holding a child's hand**-a child has passed, via miscarriage, abortion, early death.

- **White light in hands**-gift of protection for what you need to do.
- **Letters**-usually the letter of the first name of the departed spirit.
- **Numbers**-have meaning either to spirit or client, birthday, favorite number, house number, etc.
- **Hands fisted bumping**-means sudden impact, sudden death.
- **Fingers Crossed**-means a tight bond or connection from spirit to client.
- **Tapping of Body Part**-shows what part of body caused their death or where illness started.
- **Tapping wrist**-refers to a watch or bracelet.
- **Books**-school, or reference to needing more knowledge.

The messages can come in jumbled, or in a different hand-writing style. Usually there is no grammar or punctuation, and words can range from one word to complete paragraphs. As a Psychic Medium, I call only upon the loved ones for the client and for no other spirit. I write all down, the good and bad, and only the messages that are coming through. Protect yourself by asking only this for yourself or your client. If an energy feels negative or uncomfortable, you'll need to stop immediately.

Soon you'll know who is connecting with you by the words and images that are appearing. Start with short sessions and write repetitive symbols and patterns down. Evaluate them from your own perspective, and begin logging your symbols and the meanings.

At first, thoughts, symbols, images, letters, numbers and words will start to enter your mind and through your hand.

You will think you may just be thinking of these things, but soon to realize, that a spirit is actually coming through.

Automatic Writing needs to be practiced. You must relax and shift the minds, letting the subconscious receive the messages from spirit. This is so you are not thinking about what you are writing, you are just letting the information flow onto paper. Always have questions ready prior to a session. I have a standard set of questions I always ask.

Some of the questions I ask Spirit are;

- What is your name or initial of your first name?
- How did you pass?
- Where did you die?
- What specific details can you tell me for _____(clients name)?
- They are here for wanting to connect with you today, please speak with us, I am here to give them messages for you.
- What guidance or advice can you give?
- The client then will ask some questions.

When automatic writing, it is important to not think or try to interpret what you are writing as you are receiving it. You just write, and interpret afterwards. If you try to analyze while receiving the information, it will more likely block your ability, and not be a truthful message. When you are engaged in a session, you should feel calm and relaxed, open to anything that comes into mind, open to spirit. You may as I do, feel the energy of spirit, and sometimes get teary-eyed. Also, the trance feels like a daydream, light with good vibrational energy. You may feel peaceful, surrounding love, and the essence of that spirit.

You will eventually get a sense on how it 'feels' and the deciphering of what is written. It is extremely exhilarating when you connect. Accessing, higher-self, spirit guides, Divine Source, is truly amazing and continues to be for me every time.

There are other things to consider when in trance and automatic writing.

- You may SEE-colors, shapes, different light sources, blue light, white light, clothing, and animals.
- You may HEAR- sounds, music, tapping, voices, whispers.
- You may FEEL-cold, hot, warm, a spirit present in or around you, their remorse for something they are sorry for.
- You may SMELL-perfumes, flowers, smoke, food- any scent related to the spirit.

The more you practice, the better you will get. Try not to break trance when experiencing any of the above. It can take you by surprise. Try to maintain trance and focus, continuing with the messages. Let you hand and mind connect with spirit, enjoy practicing and receiving.

Automatic Writing for the Creative Individual

If you are the creative type, a writer, musician, etc., you can automatic write for help with your creativity. You can enter trance and ask for assistance for what you are working on. Many musicians, artists and writers experience divine intervention when creating. I have experienced this many times in my art, writing and music.

I am an accomplished Fine Artist, with a Fine Art Degree from F.I.T. I have been dubbed Lady Leonardo by New York News 1, and have been featured in many articles. I have done mural work that when I finished I would step back, look up and say "Thank You LORD, thank you for this talent-I can't believe I painted this." Time was always distorted, passing quickly and the results amazing to myself, not really remembering how I did it. This is "trance" state at its best.

Whether a musician, writer, singer, artist-allowing yourself to use an altered state of consciousness, frees the creative flow. Then you enter that magical state so you can connect with your inner core, divine sources-and then ultimately with audiences.

Try entering "trance" state before working on a project, or for unblocking yourself. Have paper and pen ready and allow your inner work to flow. Ask for guidance and help from the divine power. Ask for things to flow easily and effortlessly-see what happens. Most of the time when I am finished with a project, I truly can't believe how I did it. I am so deeply focused inward, turning cell phone off, thinking of nothing but what I am concentrating on. This takes practice too. But once you experience the outcomes, you will always work your creativity in this way. You can also, try this before going to sleep-but have pen and notebook handy, you will wake up writing.

Achieving heightened abilities and flow through trance, helps your creative work reach levels you never thought you could.

So, begin practicing and see how the information is being sent to you. Everyone has a different way of receiving symbols and information. The more you practice, you will notice similar signs and symbols in regard to the information. They will come in the same each time for a specific message, so you will have to learn as you go. Be patient, it can get frustrating at first, but eventually you see start to see things with more clarity. Keep in mind to always write everything that comes to mind and do not think about or analyze what is appearing on paper. You may notice the information coming through in pieces, this is quite normal. You may receive a picture, then a word, then a number...

Let your subconscious run free and evaluate after the session is completed.

It is fun to practice this with trusting friends or family members. You can do this over the phone with anyone or facetime or skype as I do for my long-distance clients.

Questions that will assist in communicating with Spirit...for others:

1. Who is with us today?
2. What is your name or initial?
3. What message can I relay to
   _____(Client's Name)
4. Is there anything that was left unfinished/unsaid?
5. Show me how you passed?
6. Where did you pass?
7. How old were you at passing?
8. Can you tell me specific details about yourself that only____ would know?
9. Can you tell me what you see from your perspective?
10. Can you tell me specific details about
    _____(Client's Name)
11. Is there something you need to tell them?

Questions to ask for yourself are very personal and will need to be written down prior to entering a light trance. Group your questions in categories; relationships/love, business/career, family issues, money/abundance requests, spiritual growth and enlightenment and anything else. This helps keep you focused on your inner awareness and not thinking of questions to ask. If you do not write questions down as a beginner, you may find yourself searching for questions; resulting in breaking trance, receiving muddled messages and losing focus and the ability to communicate.

When items, pictures, symbols and shapes come through and you do not know what they are or stand for-I suggest you ask Spirit -What is this I am drawing? This has happened many times in my sessions and an example of this is when I drew small oval/round shapes. I drew five of them, but didn't know what they were, neither did my client. I simply asked Spirit, "What are these?" and then I wrote, Pancakes. My client laughed with teary eyes and stated she had five kids and her Mom (The Spirit Guide we were communicating with) always called them her "little pancakes." *So simply ask, when you need to…*

CHAPTER 7

HOW TO BEGIN

To properly begin you will need a white candle, white computer paper, a few pens and a quiet area to relax and get comfortable. Make sure you will not be disturbed or interrupted. Turn off all cell phones, TV's, radios anything that may disrupt your meditative trance. Dedicate this space for where you practice. Decorate your table with crystals, candles, rosary beads, a talisman or amulet. My table is a 'white table" with a white tablecloth, white candles, white feathers, crystals, holy water and a rosary from "Fatima". I also have my *crystal pendulum* and answer diagram to use after the session on the table.
I love crystals and their meanings, so I add and use the elements (crystals) when doing the pendulum.
Basic information on the elements are:

- Element EARTH: Direction North   Angel Uriel
  ZODIAC: Taurus, Virgo, Capricorn
- Element AIR: Direction East   Angel
  Raphael   Libra, Aquarius, Gemini
- Element FIRE: Direction South   Angel
  Michael   Aries, Leo, Sagittarius
- Element WATER: Direction West   Angel
  Gabriel   Cancer, Scorpio, Pisces

Decorate your table in whatever way makes you feel protected, comfortable and peaceful.

At the subconscious level, each and every time you enter your spiritual place, you will automatically relax your mind and body. You are also allowing your psychic abilities to prepare to open for communication.

Whether alone or working with a friend or client, the preparation is the same.

An opening technique and prayer must be learned and used at each session before communicating with Spirit. This is personal and you will need to prepare your own individual opening prayer that you are comfortable with.

My OPENING prayer and technique steps are:

- Light candles
- Put soft meditation music on-or hypnosis music-nature sounds-whatever relaxes you
- Close eyes-Take a few deep breaths-RELAX body and mind-Focus inward-Take deep breaths -In through the nose and out through the mouth...Imagine WHITE light pouring over your head and all around you.
- Close eyes-uncross legs-then imagine roots from feet are extending below into floor, grounding oneself. Then I ask to be grounded for this session.
- PRAYER-I ask the Divine Lord, the Angels and Spirit Guides to come forth and give the messages through me. I thank you in advance and want to experience a beautiful connection for_____.
  Please send me the messages. This person is here to speak and connect with Spirit for many reasons.
  When I open my "third eye" (which is in middle of brows) please allow me to see everything I need to see, at this point imagine your third eye opening.
- Imagine a zipper on the top of your head...When I open the zipper -Please allow me to hear everything I need to hear, at this point imagine the zipper opening on your head.

- Allow information to flow…begin writing whatever comes to mind.

CLOSING

- Take a few deep breaths-In through the nose -out through the mouth
- Imagine your Zipper closing on the head
- Imagine your third eye closing
- Thank Spirit for sending messages

My students at my intuitive workshops all learn this technique and are always amazed at the success of receiving after opening properly. Follow it step by step and enjoy practicing. Some of you may receive information easier if holding an object that the departed owned and wore. This is Psychometry. Holding an item may help you receive more information. This is an individualized learning process, so try a few ways until you just *"feel"* what is working best for you to communicate.

Once the session is complete you can now review what was written on your pages. I usually have two to four pages of writings. When automatic writing for yourself you will have to wait till the session is over. If writing and receiving for someone else, you may ask during the session if the messages mean anything.
With practice you will be able to communicate with spirit and receive guidance for all areas of your life.

When I'm doing sessions for my clients I also ask spirit to body scan them for their health. Sometimes I get a message for someone to get a check-up or stay on top of their medical issues. I told one client that she was going to need surgery very soon and to prepare. Within six months she had to have surgery.

Another client I was reading asked about her health and all I saw were needles. I tell her there are lots of needles and you won't need surgery. Two months later I see her and her Doctor said to try acupuncture and she did.

PYSCHIC "CLAIRS"

Understanding where and how the information is received is important. Each person will receive psychic information differently. There are four major "Clairs", in which we receive information from spirit.

- **Clairvoyance**-*is clear vision.* You may see images, mini movies, colors, numbers and your third eye when opened allows the information in for you see. Visions while dreaming, flash visions while awake, and visions while in trance/meditation are how myself and psychics "see" information. Can be startling at times to see these visions.

- **Clairaudience**-*is clear hearing.* The sounds, music and voices will be heard within the ear. May be loud or soft.

- **Clairsentience**-*is clear sensing/feeling.* This is the ability to feel spirit, feel emotional states of others and is also part of ***Psychometry***-which is the ability to retrieve information from holding/touching objects, houses, jewelry and clothing.

Most people have experienced some sort of clairsentience. Feeling as if someone is in the room with you, maybe experiencing the sensation of being touched with no explanation. Feeling sudden temperature changes in a room with no explanation. Feeling others emotions.

- **Claircognizance**-*is clear knowing.* It is the ability to "just know" something to be true without any supporting knowledge or reason. You can't explain how you know or even where the information comes from. *I believe it to be a prophetic sense*, knowing future events, knowing things will work out...You "just know". Claircognizant people just seem to have an answer for everything, just knowing.

They just know where missing objects are. Can read people easily. Are creative individuals. Constantly thinking, learning and a collector of information.

- **Clairalience-***is clear smelling.* This is the fifth "clair" that I also have. Receiving specific psychic information based on smells. Your ability to smell the odor of the person who has passed, or their perfume. Smells of smoke, food, spices, flowers and any odors that spirit may have been around in their human life.

Clairalience Story #1
One morning, my sister Denise and I both smelled the exact perfume my Mom used to wear- at the same time. My sister lives in Arizona and I in New Jersey. She called me to ask if anything strange happened and I said yes, mom came to visit-she said she visited me too-I smelled her perfume, I said so did I.

Truly amazing to experience the "clairs". The more you practice and develop your psychic skills, the more information can come through in all of the above ways.

Clairalience Story #2
I was doing a reading on my dear friend Lydia. Her mother came through and she was amazed, for she said her mom never comes. I started *smelling oranges* and asked her

what's with oranges-I smell oranges. Lydia thinks for a moment and can't recall anything pertaining to oranges and her mother. So, I continue with the reading and then it's back...the smell of oranges...I say to Lydia, I really smell oranges and your mom is sending this message through smell...she is showing me oranges and I'm smelling them.

A few minutes had passed, Lydia is amazed and tells me - YES-I just starting putting an orange by my bedside to eat instead of getting up and having a cookie!

This is how Spirit communicates to show what they see, they watch over us, and the message keeps coming back until the meaning is found.

When automatic writing, the information will come in many different ways, and you just write whatever it is your sensing, hearing, seeing, smelling, knowing...It is exhilarating and enlightening. Remembering to *only communicate* with your loved ones, Divine Power (God) and your Angels.

I often get teary-eyed or even cry with my clients-as I feel Spirit-and sense the emotion they are sending. Many of my clients ask, "Can you see what they look like?", sometimes I can, and sometimes I just see light forms. Quite interesting and moving.

It's important to know the questions you want to ask of spirit. I have said this before, but it is crucial to developing your skills and to allow information to flow easily, without interruption of searching for questions, or letting the conscious mind take control. The subconscious mind needs to be open and accessible. Write 10-15 questions down that you will always ask spirit when practicing your automatic writing. This will help you to form a pattern that will become natural. As you go, you will revise your questions, start to understand your abilities and create a comfortable format that works for you.

Being aware of all your senses takes practice also. You can work on them (the clairs) one at a time with each session you try and see which is stronger and which is weaker. I recommend you continue practicing with your strong "clairs" first until you get a clear understanding of the process. Then move on to tuning in to your other senses and work on them.

There are certain common causes that would *awaken your psychic abilities*-naturally.

- **NDE-Near Death Experience**-Many stories of people in near-fatal accidents, comas, serious injuries that cause momentary death-begin to have psychic experiences. Catching a glimpse of the other side, being greeted by an Angel, Spirit, or God himself. They are awakened and it is profoundly life changing.

- **LOSING LOVED ONES**-When a loved one passes, a spiritual awakening occurs. When confronted by death we begin to evaluate our own existence and our own life is deepened. We may get a sign, see something unexplainable or have a dream where psychic awakenings occur. Never-the less, death can bring us closer to our spirituality, show us the true path to journey and amazing self-discovery.

As a psychic medium, I've seen death before it happens. I dreamt my husband's death one night, in full detail. It was horrendous and I simply could not remove the images. I woke many times, crying, sweating and wondering why I am seeing such a terrible accident. At the end of the dream I heard a phone ringing and I answered and heard a male voice say, "There's been a terrible accident." I woke up for the third time and stayed up. It was painful to see these images and to feel like it was real.

He was in Florida, I in New York and the next day I asked him to be careful throughout the day. He said, "Why-did you dream something?" I didn't want to tell him what I dreamt-but did tell him to be careful.
The day was great and I spoke to him around 3:00pm. He was off to play poker and said he would call me later that evening. Our usual goodbye, love you and talk later. At 9:30pm that evening I get a phone call, and a male voice says, "There's been a terrible accident-is someone home with you?" I instantly had a flash of the horrendous visions from the night before. The officer went on to say it was fatal.

Moving forward in time...I was truly upset that I could not change this. Even having the premonition of it. I was mad at the other side and felt I never got an answer why I would see such things and then not be able to alter them-UNTIL I saw my Mother's death. I saw her gravely ill and passing for months. My visions in my dream state were showing me this over and over again. My mother was living in Arizona near my two sisters at the time and she seemed to have been in remission. I'm sleeping peacefully one night only to be *awakened by an Angel* telling me my mother was going to die Friday that week.

I called my brother who lives in Manhattan to tell him this and to book a flight immediately. He has witnessed my psychic abilities and instantly booked our flights. My sisters couldn't believe we were flying in-they knew I knew

81

something. I told them when we arrived that I heard an Angel tell me she would die Friday. They said she was rushed into the hospital and kept asking for me. I promised my Mother I would hold her hand and be with her when she passes. I slept at the hospital for two nights and yes- she passed on that Friday, October 25, 2013 – as I held her hand.

I'm grateful to have these psychic abilities-to be aware, in tune, to receive and then act accordingly, with full belief and faith that I am guided and connected to Divine Power (God), Angels and Spirit at all times. If I weren't- I may have missed my Mother's passing.

- **HEALING MODALITIES**-such as; Hypnosis and Reiki can open-up individuals to the spiritual world through clearing the chakras and to shifting the awareness-allowing the subconscious mind to be open and accessible during a session.

As a Clinical Hypnotherapist, many of my clients experience a psychic awakening while in hypnosis. They sometimes hear their name being called by spirit. They see their loved ones. They feel them being touched by Spirit. They shed happy tears and awaken from "trance" truly changed, relieved, with an overwhelming feeling of love and peace.

I like to keep a journal by my bed to write things down if awakened during the night with visions, or thoughts. I have received much information during my sleep. On the creative side of psychic awareness, you can dream poems, songs, see glimpses of your future, and all the positive things that lie ahead. This is highly beneficial in making decisions in the present to attain what you may have seen in your future.

When I am giving a reading and automatic writing session, I do see people's future events. They can then act upon and adjust their decisions to those visions in a positive way. This is for all areas of life. Whether it's; relationships, career paths, moving, marriage, etc. the information at least makes you think about your present choices.

So, begin your journey practicing and experiencing automatic "trance" writing, psychic awakenings and the amazing information you can and will receive to help you in all areas of your life. The knowing you can rely on Spiritual sources for information is truly enlightening and will free you of fear, self-doubt, and bring confidence, empowerment and overall peace. Everything will seem to just be more calm, relaxed, effortless, and the "allowing" of things to happen naturally and its own pace, eliminates worry and stress.

Be patient and practice. The more you practice the easier it will be to receive messages. Embrace your new knowledge and explore.

A few other common causes and reasons that may enhance and awaken your psychic abilities are:

- Outer Body Experience (OBE)
- Near Death Experience (NDE)
- A healing, A Miracle, an unexplainable outcome
- Illness, trauma, accidents
- Past Life Regression Therapy
- Desire and heightened need to be away from negativity

- Overwhelming passion to learn and be more Spiritual
- Frequent and vivid dreams-(that happen-days-weeks-months later)
- Heightened Sensitivity of "All" your senses.
- Practicing intuitiveness
- Shift in awareness that you are a spiritual being
- Cleansed from external debris, pollution, free from fear
- Clearing and balancing of the Chakras

CHAPTER 8

AUTOMATIC WRITING & PSYCHOMETRY PAIRING

In the paranormal world, there are many ways to communicate with the other side and each person will have better results with some ways than others. Another way to help assist in communicating with spirit is to hold an object that belonged to them, that had meaning, something they wore such as; jewelry, clothing. Best to use something that was worn daily than something that was just owned and worn infrequently. The object retains energy from the person and then psychically you read the object. Information may come easier to you through this method. By holding an object of the deceased person, you may be able to sense the history of it, receiving residual information as words, colors, images or sensations. Finding out who owned it, where they got it, and validating the information from the person who may know the history.

You can prepare for automatic writing and then hold an object to see if it helps you more with receiving information. When holding the item, simply allow whatever comes to mind to be written down. If you feel sensations write what you are feeling, if you hear something, see an image, letter, number, just write it all down. If you smell anything-write what you smell. You may receive information more rapidly by adding the object so be ready.

This is a lot of fun to practice with friends. You can all get together and each person brings an item from a loved one (alive or passed) then put items on a table and everyone picks one to read. Spend a half hour with the item then discuss what was written and felt. Each person will be able to validate anything that was communicated on the item they brought.

If you have psychometric abilities, then you would be able to get information about the person who owned the item, or how the item was used, or the event of where and how the item became the property of the owner. If you are a psychic, you would then be able to retrieve more detailed information about the person who owned the item, maybe how they died, and what the item meant to the person.

Vibrations and emotions are the two components that are left and remain imprinted on items. It's as if the items hold a wealth of information, a story, that is embedded in the item, the aura, the energy field around the item. I believe that it's the combination of both the item carrying remaining energy, along with spirit communicating information about the item. Some psychics ask their clients to bring photos, jewelry, clothing, any item the person owned to assist in the reading.

I recall someone bringing a ring to one of my reading sessions. I held the ring and it looked like a ring a female would wear. I held it for a few moments, and stated that a man wore this ring, and he loved it even though it did seem a little feminine. Also, he bought it on a trip and always wore it since that day. My client laughed and said it was kind of a test. Her father did wear it, and she validated the story to be correct. This is why you must always go with your inner guidance, listen to the first information to come about, and not think-but let the subconscious work to receive truthful information. Anyone new at this and practicing would more likely think it was owned by a female based on just the look of the ring, but you are reading an item through the subconscious level; not studying the actual item and then basing information on the conscious level.

Best to not look at an item – just hold it first and wait to see what you get.

How to Practice and Begin Psychometry & Automatic Writing

1. Find an area for your psychic work. Be sure it will be quiet and with least distractions and noise as possible. Best to always use the same area.
2. You can put background tonal music on, reiki music, hypnotic music, whatever helps you to meditate, go inward, enter trance.
3. Set your space up spiritually. Crystals, incense, candles, etc.
4. Relax and sit comfortably. Close eyes.
5. Always open your psychic awareness with a prayer of protection. Then open your third-eye chakra. Picture the third-eye between your brows and see it opening.
6. Touch lightly and in a circular motion the hand that will be holding the object. This is to awaken your sense of touch.
7. Try to be handed the item with your eyes closed so that you do not see the actual item. Nothing should be said about the item.
8. Allow your senses to take over, let any images, sounds, smells, appear in whatever way they come. You can say what you see, or begin to write it

down. Some images will be very detailed and some may be vague. You're not to think about what you are picking up, you just relay the messages as is; without editing on your part. It's not your place to analyze or interpret what makes sense.

9. Close your session with another prayer, thanking spirit, and shutting down your third eye.

The theory about psychometry is that all thoughts, events, and actions leave impressions on just about everything. With this belief, you can understand that psychics/mediums/psychometrists can be quite helpful in finding not just missing items, but missing persons. Forensic psychics have been known to be extremely helpful in; murder cases, missing persons, and examining items such as; weapons, clothing, any item left at a scene to help with a case. Take time to read about some of the amazing cases that were solved with the help of a forensic psychic.

During any type of psychic session, whether it be automatic writing, psychometry, "clair" readings, mediumship, be aware that the images may not be so pleasant. It takes a special psychic to do forensic work, but just the same, doing any psychic work allows for all information-good and bad to be communicated. I have psychically seen during my sessions; deaths, suicides of all types, visions of accidents and the way the person died, and so on. It can be disturbing at times, but very helpful to the person you are reading.

One disturbing psychic medium session that I always think of is when a young male in his 20's told me what happened and how he died. He took medicine, drank a beer, and went to lay down on the couch. I saw images of him resting, but then I saw him choking on his vomit. I was disturbed by this, but was telling my client what I was seeing. He said yes, that's him and that did happen. Spirit kept saying it was an accident-not suicide.

Another session that was memorable was when a female spirit came through and showed me the entire scene of her suicide. She kept telling me she sat all day in her car. I saw a hospital building and a garage. She waited and waited to tell me more-just showing me how she sat for hours. Then in the vision she gets out of the car and walks towards the half wall overlooking the street. Then I see her gone. I tell the client this and tell her I feel she jumped. I can't see the jump-but she's gone and I feel she jumped. The client is crying and said yes, she jumped and she did wait all day in her car.

When accessing your psychic abilities, you are open to all information. Experiment with automatic writing, psychometry, and see what helps you most in receiving information from spirit. You can also read items to receive information about living people. Being a Psychic means you use your "Clairs" to get information for the present and future life of an individual. Being a Medium means you speak and communicate with spirit. Being Psychic doesn't mean you are a Medium, but a Medium is both. I do both Medium and Psychic readings with automatic writing combined. It's fascinating to both myself and my clients.

SUGGESTED ITEMS FOR PSYCHOMETRY

- Photos-any/all that are relative to the reading.
- Walls-Touch walls if on location.
- Furniture-where they sat, ate, used.

- Jewelry-that they wore, try not to read second hand jewelry-this will have other imprints from previous owners.
- Clothing-something worn all the time, favorite sweater, scarf, etc.
- Toys-if child passed, or collection item.
- Any item that has sentimental value!

So, have fun experimenting and learning what works best for you. It takes practice, but you will begin to get better at it and receive more and more information with each session. Remember to open and close properly with prayer and to just let the information flow into your subconscious and onto paper!

Practice giving psychic readings, reading items, and connecting with spirit -with friends and family. They can also hide an item, and you can try to use your psychic abilities to see where it is. It's fun and will work your psychic muscles. You can get a group together and just let information flow in and ask them as a group who the messages are for.

If you are serious about learning and expanding your Psychic awareness and development, you may want to take a psychic development course, or seek out a mentor. A good psychic coach will expand your gifts beyond your own self-taught methods. The biggest issue is trusting the information that is coming through and relaying it properly. Also, understanding and learning your symbols and what they stand for.

I teach Psychic development courses and love when my clients begin to receive messages. They learn and understand the "Clairs" and discover which are their strong ones. Life changes for them, they see things differently, hear, feel, and sense a new spiritual life and connection that is quite profound and amazing.

CHAPTER 9

CLEAR INTENTIONS

When working on your psychic abilities and development you need to be clear of negativity, from your own thoughts and from outside sources. Negativity will block you from receiving truthful information. If you are depressed, on medication, or use any other altering substances, I don't recommend developing or practicing any psychic skills. A negative or altered state of mind can bring unwanted spirit and more negativity to you.

It's most important to be clear of negative attitudes also. People, friends, family, spouses that doubt you and are negative about your psychic work will only make it more difficult for you to develop your intuitiveness. To be able to communicate with spirit (Medium), give psychic readings (Psychic), Automatic "Trance" Write, or work through Pyschometry, you MUST set and have clear intentions. This is the proper and safe way to communicate, receive information and keep only positivity around you.

To raise my vibration and open my "clairs" and to the spiritual world, I start with a prayer and with *clear intentions* on whom I'm calling upon, whom I'm reading, and for the reason of healing and giving a needed message.

Example:

"Dear God, Angels, and Spirit Guides, please allow me to hear and see messages from only those loved ones who have crossed over for _____(Client name). Please send what they need, they are here for a reason and I am an open and clear channel for them. I trust what you send.

Also, the client can pray silently with you for their loved ones to come through.

The energy and vibration around you should shift. You may feel lighter, feel energy within and around you. This is normal. As the psychic reading and automatic writing begins and continues, you continue with clear intentions on what you need for your client and for the validity of the reading. I ask for names, initials, how they passed. I ask for them to let me know what they see as they watch over. This means, I am sent information on what the client has been doing, or events that are forthcoming etc. This includes things that I could never know, such as abuse within a marriage, divorce, arrests, substance abuse, and suicides. I never know what I messages I will be receiving -so I am just as surprised to give them as they are receiving them. *An authentic Psychic/Medium* has little or no control over what will be communicated through them.

I always continue asking for details for the client, and for specific information they would only know. I am tested from time to time by clients, and I love when the session is completed. I have made many skeptics leave crying, baffled and believers.

Clear Intentions for both medium work and psychic work are extremely important for the client and for you and your business. When giving psychic readings, you are giving information for their life path, purpose, health, career, love life and more...It's truthful information through the subconscious that needs to be communicated and not conscious evaluation. Do not rush and get into trance state or meditative state when doing your psychic work.

Whether practicing for yourself, to read others, to learn about psychic development, to advance your psychic skills, or to just understand how a psychic or medium works, these tips should be helpful;

1. Be open to receive what you need, NOT what you want. The messages may not be what you want to hear. If you expect a certain answer or message, you may be disappointed.
2. The psychic/medium guides the sessions. The client can ask questions, but minimal talking from the client is required for an *authentic reading*. During a session, the psychic/medium will ask for validation of the information being conveyed.
3. Specific details should come through that only the person being read would know. Something odd or strange, a nickname, a specific item they were given, etc.

It's normal for people to have recall problems and to have a delayed response to the information being told to them. I often get text messages days and weeks later from clients realizing what some of their messages meant. One session my client forgot her own Mother's name. I wrote it while automatic writing and asked if she knew anyone by that name...she said no, only minutes later to say -YES-that's my Mom's name. I explain at the beginning of my sessions that sometimes this will happen.

It's important to keep calm and wait for the client to absorb information at their own pace.

4. A Psychic will give you intuitive information through their psychic "Clairs". The information is for your life, relationships, health, abundance, career, purpose, and future.
5. A Medium will connect with those loved ones who have passed, and receive messages from them-then conveyed to you. A medium is also psychic, but a psychic is not a medium.

    I am a Medium. When I give a session, I first connect and communicate with spirit. My psychic "clair" reading then come afterwards. I also automatic write throughout the entire session.

6. An authentic reading will feel wonderful, enlightening, touching and memorable. It should bring the client some peace, balance, a healing, and an overall amazing experience.

I love being a Psychic Medium! I enjoy meeting so many wonderful people (and their loved ones who have passed.) It's extremely rewarding to help people connect to spirit, to get insight for their life, future and to heal. Authentic Mediums are highly spiritual and work with Divine Power, Angels and Spirit Guides. Never anything negative or dark. I feel wonderful and enlightened during and after every session.

A psychic medium can also receive warning messages, such as; to drive with caution, rethink a situation, to do or not do something, to seek medical care, all with intent to protect or guide the person towards a more positive outcome. I have been warned a few times for my own life. Some through dreams, some warnings I heard instantly before an accident happened that I could have been in. But, I hear, see and then act upon those messages-allowing to receive protection. There are different levels of psychic abilities, and it can take time to allow oneself to be open at all times to receive what you need, yet stay focused on life itself. I allow my psychic "clairs" to be open all the time, but my mediumship is turned on and off with each session.

In closing, I want everyone to understand that we are all capable of developing psychic skills. Take it seriously and practice your new skills.

- Practice alone, or with a partner and allow yourself to go inward and to enter "trance"-to allow the subconscious to receive messages, information, warnings, protection, guidance and healing.

- Keep negativity out of your circle, and only keep positive influences, thoughts and actions within and around you.

- Enjoy setting up your spiritual psychic area of work. White candles, crystals, holy water, and Angel statues are some of the items I have. Find what makes you feel protected, open, peaceful and balanced.

- Open and Close properly. Write your opening and closing to what you "feel" is comfortable for you.

- Only write and speak exactly what comes through you...NOTHING more-NOTHING less. Do not think about what is coming through-just allow it to and evaluate later. This is the hardest thing to learn.

Practice until you are extremely comfortable and confident before working with others. If you feel you are ready to read others, start with friends who support you. It takes confidence in your skills to say you are a psychic or medium. You are as good as your readings…word of mouth creates clientele and a loyal following.

If you are wanting to only learn this for your own guidance for your life, then every day spend 30 minutes to an hour on your psychic skills. Tune in for your own answers, guidance, future, and any messages that you may receive. It's up to you to act upon what you have been sent, it's your choice to listen or not to. Your inner awareness, guidance system, psychic intuitiveness, divine power, angels and spirit guides will always lead you toward a truthful path and positive place. I have always listened and always ended up better than I could ever imagined.

Place a journal by your bedside, for many messages and spirit come through the dream state. Ask before sleeping; any questions you need answers to, for any messages to come through, or for a visit by a spirit guide or angel. Open yourself before sleeping and see what you recall when you awake.

Whether for yourself or others, I want everyone to know and realize that the power is within all of us. We all have intuitiveness, some need to be awakened, some need to learn it, some have it naturally. Experiencing life with your mind and spirit opened to the divine power, the universe, angels, spirit guides and psychic senses will benefit you in many ways all through your life. You will always have guidance from the most powerful sources and feel a sense of peace, calmness, a knowing that you can trust what you are sent.

- Trust your psychic senses, trust the divine power, the universe.
- Tune in and listen to your inner wisdom and guidance system. Spirit speaks through you.
- Trust the source and yourself to accomplish dreams and goals, to connect for guidance, strength, and healing, for all areas in your life.
- Eliminate fear and realize the power of faith and the power within you.

The power of prayer and communication with spirit is available to all of us – all of the time!

ABOUT THE AUTHOR

Please visit the website at
www.SpiritualMediumGinaCannone.com or
www.GCHypnotherapy.com

Email: artist_gina@msn.com

LOVE & LIGHT TO ALL

Made in the USA
San Bernardino, CA
29 July 2020